YESTERDAY IN SANTA FE

YESTERDAY
IN
SANTA FE
Episodes in a Turbulent History

Marc Simmons

SUNSTONE PRESS

For Sarah and Kit

Revised Edition / Second Printing

Printed in the United States of America

Library of Congress Cataloging in Publication Data:

Simmons, Marc.
     Yesterday in Santa Fe.

     Bibliography: p.
     Includes index.
     1. Santa Fe (N.M.)--History. I. Title.
F804.S245S56   1987   978.9'56   87-6449
ISBN: 0-86534-108-7

Published by   SUNSTONE PRESS
                   Post Office Box 2321
                   Santa Fe, NM 87504-2321 / USA

CONTENTS

Preface...7

Yesterday in Santa Fe................................9

The Naming of Santa Fe..............................10

An Unseemly Feud....................................16

Of Love-Potions and Witchcraft......................22

Reckoning in Blood..................................24

The First Urban Renewal.............................29

A Remarkable Celebration............................32

The Earliest Municipal Code.........................35

A Governor Loses His Head...........................38

A Crooked Derby.....................................41

New Branches of the Tree............................45

"Telegraph" Aubry: A Riding Man.....................48

Bishop Lamy's Hairbreadth Escape....................51

Murder Most Atrocious...............................53

The Coming of the Railroad, 1880....................56

Violence in Politics................................58

Santa Fe Burros.....................................61

A Postscript..69

A Santa Fe Chronology...............................70

A Note on Sources...................................71

Index...73

PREFACE

"The best thing we derive from history," said Goethe, "is the enthusiasm it raises in us." Which is just another way of saying, history is to be enjoyed. And it is principally to this end that the following episodes have been written and are offered to all those who have some interest in Santa Fe as it used to be.

Many people believe that history is instructive, agreeing with Santayana's dictum that those who fail to learn from the past are condemned to repeat it. But the lessons of history are never self-evident; they remain open to a variety of interpretation and to misinterpretation. For example, to the earliest Anglo-American traders venturing over the Santa Fe Trail, New Mexico's captial appeared to be a shabby collection of mud huts clustered along narrow, dust-laden streets. And the population seemed timid and lacking in industry. Such observations filled the traders' chronicles and helped shape a negative stereotype that remained current for decades.

But a closer look and a less prejudiced assessment would have revealed to the Yankee merchants that an adobe building was well-suited to the place and the climate. Earth and straw for the bricks was plentiful. Abundant solar energy insured speedy drying and curing. And since no great skill was required either in the manufacture or laying up of bricks in the wall, the most humble family could possess a substantial dwelling. Moreover, a house of adobe was cool in summer and could be made warm in winter by feeding juniper and piñon sticks to the corner fireplace.

Many skeptical Americans, in fact, were won over in the years that followed their arrival, finding that a mud house had its advantages as well as a measure of ingratiating charm.

They were also forced to revise their opinions of Santa Fe's native inhabitants. Hospitality came as natural to the New Mexicans as did their light-heartedness during a fiesta or fandango. With a limited technology, they nevertheless managed to feed themselves and provide some comforts in the household by careful utilization of available resources. And with primitive weapons they heroically defended themselves from marauding Indians.

Descendants of Santa Fe's pioneer citizenry still display these traits of friendliness, ingenuity, and endurance. And many of them, possessed of enterprise, have risen to positions of leadership in today's political, social, cultural, and business community.

Each of the little essays presented herein opens a small window on some aspect of life in New Mexico's ancient capital. Taken together, they form a kind of loose history covering a period of 350 years. The details of a number of these stories have long been familiar to historians but have not been available to a wider audience since they were tucked away in obscure corners. Several of the pieces offer wholly new information, representing original research on the part of the author. For the curious, a brief note at the end of the volume will explain the sources of the author's information.

For assistance in preparation of this book, thanks are extended to E.W. Tedlock, Jr., Dr. Myra Ellen Jenkins formerly of the New Mexico State Records Center and Archives, Dr. David Weber, Dr. John Kessell, Susie Henderson, and Frank Turley.

Marc Simmons
Los Cerrillos, New Mexico

YESTERDAY IN SANTA FE

Tewa Indians were probably the first people to inhabit the site of modern Santa Fe. Vestiges of their pueblos were evident until recent times, and even now excavations within the limits of the city produce archaeological proof of this earlier occupation. Fairly extensive ruins remain down the Santa Fe River near the community of Agua Fria, Pindi Pueblo on the north side of the stream being one of the larger sites. Indians from this area, no doubt farmed up river, using the arable flat lands now occupied by the city. They also must have had trails leading from their adobe villages along the length of the valley into the foothills of the Sangre de Cristo Mountains. We know very little about these original inhabitants, because when the Spaniards arrived in the sixteenth century, they found the banks of the Santa Fe River deserted.

Francisco Vásquez de Coronado, who made the earliest and most extensive reconaissance of New Mexico in the years 1540–1542, was once thought to have left a small group of followers behind, mostly Mexican Indians, who established an informal settlement on the Santa Fe location. After this story was proved a myth, the popular belief arose that Juan de Oñate had been the true founder about the year 1608. Certainly Oñate was a likely candidate for the honor, as he had been responsible for the formal colonization of New Mexico beginning in 1598. However, it is now known that that the only town he organized was the short-lived Villa of San Gabriel, situated near the Indian Pueblo of San Juan at the junction of the Chama River and the Rio Grande. Governor Pedro de Peralta, Oñate's successor, was, in fact, the man who laid the foundations for Santa Fe early in 1610.

♦—◦ ONE-THIRD OF ONE THOUSAND YEARS. ◦—♦

1550 ——⚡ The Santa Fe Tertio-Millennial Anniversary Celebration 1883
AND GRAND MINING AND INDUSTRIAL EXPOSITION

—WILL BE HELD AT—

SANTA FE, NEW MEXICO,

MONDAY, JULY 2D, TO FRIDAY, AUGUST 3D, INCLUSIVE.

THE NAMING OF SANTA FE
A HISTORICAL PROBLEM

Santa Feans traditionally have been enthusiastic about joining in celebrations of all kinds: fiestas, historical anniversaries, jubilees, and religious holidays. At such events, which combine solemnity with merry-making, the city's Hispanic heritage is reaffirmed and the people establish a personal link with their long and colorful past.

One of the most glittering and ambitious commemorative events ever staged in the old capital took place in the summer of 1883. The date 1550 had arbitrarily been agreed upon as the year of Santa Fe's founding (nothing was known at this time of the community's origin), which meant that as of 1883, she had reached the respectable age of 333 years or a third of millennium. Accordingly, elaborate plans were formulated for a "Tertio-Millenial" celebration.

One July 2 the festivities began and continued for six weeks. Beneath a sparkling sky, all citizens turned out in their finest raiment to view seemingly endless processions, parades, and historical pageants. The center of the celebration was located at present Federal Place, with the oval surrounding the grounds staked out as a race track. Here horse, mule and burro contests were run, and U.S. Cavalry units engaged in competitive drills and presented displays of fine horsemanship. For the more sanguinary spectator there were chicken pulls and cockfights. And in one splendid extravaganza, Coronado and his men fought a staged battle with rebellious Indians. Numerous Pueblo Indians, as well as members of other tribes, had been invited to participate in the commemorative activities, and in native dress they mingled in the streets with citizens arrayed as conquistadores, Spanish soldiers, mountain men, and cowboys.

A local newspaper welcomed the thousands of visitors who "had assembled to do honor to the earliest seat of western civilization" and ended with the laudatory declaration that no other exhibition in the country could equal that of Santa Fe in originality of design and in unique character.

Since recent research has shown that Santa Fe actually was established some sixty years after 1550, a tertio-millenial observance should properly have been celebrated in 1943. This information perhaps would have held slight importance to the earlier enthusiasts, since they were determined to promote some kind of historical display and would, doubtless, have devised an even more extraordinary excuse for carrying out their designs in 1883.

The incident does serve to call attention to the fact that in spite of an unusual public interest, the early history of Santa Fe has been poorly known and often inaccurately represented. In fact, it was not until 1929 that there was brought to light the document instructing Governor Peralta to move the original Oñate settlers from San Gabriel to a new villa. While this order contained precise directions for laying out the proposed town and the creation of a municpal government, nothing was said about the name which was to grace the new community. And to this day, the problem remains, for in no document now known can there be found the slightest reference as to the manner in which Santa Fe received its name.

When one surveys the documentary material available, it becomes evident that buried deep and almost lost to view are a few scraps of information that may serve as clues to the unravelling of the puzzle. To begin, we must return to Spain itself. Toward the end of the fifteenth century, Ferdinand and Isabel, nicknamed the Catholic Monarchs, personally took the field to command their armies in the final battles with the infidel Moors. That was the culmination of almost seven centuries of conflict, which had begun when the followers of Islam poured out of North Africa and almost inundated the Iberian Peninsula in the year 711. Slowly but resolutely, the Christian Spaniards fought their way southward, until by the opening of the decade of the 1490's, the Moors had been confined to their last small kingdom of Granada and their capital, the city of Granada, placed under heavy siege.

The presence of the King and Queen in the Christian camp indicated their keen interest in the achievement of ultimate victory and served at the same time to inspire the troops. The royal family, the nobility, as well as the army were lodged in a number of fine pavilions and tents on a plain six miles west of the walls of Granada. Late one night a gust of wind knocked over an oil lamp and soon flames were racing throughout the encampment. Queen Isabel and her children narrowly escaped death, and although no lives were lost a great amount of property in jewelry, silver, silks, and brocade was destroyed.

To prevent such a disaster from happening again and to provide comfortable winter quarters for the army, plans were immediately assembled for the building of a new and substantial town. For this work, soldiers were suddenly converted into stone masons, carpenters, and artisans, and in less than three months the new city appeared. It was built in the form of a walled Roman camp with a spacious plaza and regular streets crossing each other at right angles, quite unlike the confined and shapeless medieval cities then characteristic of Spain. When the labor was completed, the army asked that it be named in honor of the Queen, but Isabel modestly declined this tribute and bestowed on the place the title of Santa Fe (Holy Faith), in token of the unshaken trust manifested by her troops in Divine Providence.

So formidable was the city of Santa Fe de Granada in appearance that the Moors lost all hope of the enemy ever abandoning the siege, and within a short time they opened negotiations for the surrender of their last stronghold. Santa Fe thus became a symbol to all Spaniards of the strength of both their religion and government. Since in this same city, Columbus signed his contract which led to the discovery of the New World, Santa Fe also became inextricably connected to the fortunes of America. This link was reinforced when the Spanish rulers later decreed that cities established in the new dominions should be organized on the Roman "grid plan" after the manner of Santa Fe, since this scheme had proved highly efficient and desirable. Thus, what had begun as the military encampment of Ferdinand and Isabel soon became the model for all cities and towns raised throughout the Spanish Empire.

In Mexico as the conquistadors pushed the frontier northward against the opposition of nomadic Indians, they drew a parallel between their own experiences and the crusading efforts of their grandfathers in Spain. Were they not fighting against the infidels to spread Christianity and extend the realm of their sovereign, just as their forebearers had done in the long struggle with the Moors? As if to bear this out, the earliest Spaniards in New Mexico alluded frequently to the similarity between the Indians encountered and the people of Islam they had known in the Old World. Some of the natives here, they said, used bows like the Moors, others painted (tattooed?) their chins in the fashion of the Moorish women, and the Pueblos worshipped in underground chambers which the chroniclers called mosques, meaning, of course, the ceremonial kivas. Thus, when the Spaniards came to settle the upper Rio Grande Valley the heroic events surrounding the reconquest of Spain from the Moors were still very much in their minds, even though Granada had fallen to the Christian armies more than a century before. Certainly the first colonists here, in odd moments of reflection, could see themselves as a new breed of crusader, using the sword and the cross to win pagans to the true faith. Under the circumstances what could have been more natural than to name their capital, Santa Fe, honoring both their Holy Faith and the most cherished city in Spain.

The possibility that Santa Fe, New Mexico was named for her sister city in Spain does not seem to have occurred to historians — at least it is not mentioned in the general histories of the state. Admittedly, the evidence is thin and quite circumstantial, but surveying it leads to the conclusion that no better explanation exists at present.

According to Spanish law, the man responsible for the founding of a new municipality received the privilege of bestowing an appropriate name upon it. In the case of New Mexico's capital, that would have been Governor Pedro de Peralta who, as we've seen, was issued instructions to concentrate the original settlers in a new town or villa. This order was issued in March of 1609, but since Peralta did not reach New Mexico and take up the duties of his office until late in that year, it has generally been assumed that the construction of the villa which became Santa Fe did not get underway until the spring of 1610.

When work began, a large rectangular space was marked off for the *plaza mayor,* this to serve as the hub of the community and a parade ground for the soldiers, and straight parallel streets in the grid form were designated, along which lots to the new citizens were assigned. Grounds facing the plaza were reserved for public buildings or for residences of important persons. Along the north side was placed the Casa Real, known now as the Governors Palace, a low unpretentious structure where the chief political officers lived and had their offices. Here too were shops, work-rooms, and on the southeast corner, a round tower which served as a military chapel. A town council hall called the *cabildo* and containing a jail also faced the plaza, where a gibbet and whipping post were erected. Land was set aside for a church in the center of town, and on the south side of the Santa Fe River, a chapel called San Miguel was built to minister to the needs of the Indian servants of the Spaniards. Within time, it seems, some kind of defensive wall was added to protect the villa.

From a broad view, it is clear that Governor Peralta in arranging the plan of Santa Fe was following, though somewhat loosely, the precedent established at Santa Fe de Granada, which had become the standard for Spanish cities erected throughout America. This in itself might have been sufficient to evoke the idea of naming the town after its prototype in Spain.

And yet there is another situation which might have brought this suggestion to Peralta's mind. When Coronado entered New Mexico in 1540, one of the first Indian pueblos he saw was the Zuni town of Hawikuh, which he called Granada, partly because it seemed to resemble that Spanish city, but also to honor his sponsor, the Viceroy of Mexico, who was a native of Granada. In all events, the name became associated with Coronado's discoveries and was soon applied to all the province of New Mexico, instead of a single pueblo as he had intended. The perpetuation of this error can probably be laid to the Spanish writer Francisco López de Gómara who included an account of the Coronado expedition and mention of Granada in his *Historia General de las Indias* published in Spain in 1552. Within a short time the *Historia* had gone through fifteen editions and had been translated into English, French, and Italian. Cosmographers of these nationalities must have absorbed the account, for by the end of the sixteenth century, their maps began to designate the northern frontier of Mexico as the Kingdom of New Mexico or New Granada, or simply as Granada. And this practice was to contiue for several hundred years!

Did Pedro de Peralta see some of these early maps and was he aware that his province of New Mexico was being labelled "unofficially" New Granada? If so, no more appropriate name for the capital could have been selected than Santa Fe. Unfortunately, in the years following its founding, no Spaniard, so far as is known, ever referred to the town as Santa Fe de Nueva Granada or Santa Fe de Granada which would have helped to show that the name of the new city was definitely tied to that of the old. (The title Santa Fe de Granada [New Mexico] does appear, however, on the French-produced Coronelli map of 1680.) But practically all colonial writers who had actual epxerience in New Mexico used the simple designation Villa de Santa Fe and nothing more. Notwithstanding, from what has been said, the possibility seems good that, in name at least, Santa Fe of New Mexico was the offspring of Santa Fe of Granada.

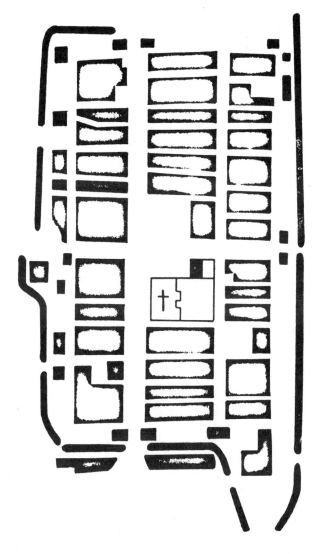

Plan of Santa Fe (Granada), Spain.

AN UNSEEMLY FEUD

In the great wagon caravan that travelled from Mexico City to the province of New Mexico in the year 1612, there was included a group of friars of the Franciscan Order coming to aid their brothers already in the field in the conversion of the Pueblo Indians. Numbered among these missionaries was one Fr. Isidro Ordóñez, a man of long service on this frontier, who only the year before had journeyed south to seek aid and recruits for the Church's work. As he trudged up the Rio Grande Valley through the wagon dust and the heat of mid-summer, Father Ordóñez felt a sense of smug satisfaction. Not only was he bearing much needed supplies and introducing a fresh contingent of workers to convert the heathen, but he also carried among his personal belongings a letter elevating him to the post of commissary or prelate in charge of the New Mexican missions.

At Santo Domingo Pueblo where Father Ordóñez subsequently installed himself and which, in effect, became New Mexico's ecclesiastical capital, a chapter meeting was called so that the new commissary might establish his authority, issue instructions, and distribute supplies. Very quickly at this gathering Ordóñez gave hints of the stern hand he would exercise in the future. His arrogant manner alienated many of the friars who particularly resented his ill-treatment of Father Alonso Peinado, the man Ordóñez was replacing as commissary. Peinado's feelings were so ruffled at the lack of respect accorded him that he betook himself to the far eastern frontier and began the conversion of the Tiwa Indians beyond the Manzano mountains. The distress of the missionaries increased when the suspicion arose that the papers displayed by Ordóñez designating him commissary and representative of the Holy Office of the Inquisition were not genuine and that, in fact, he had forged them himself. By appeasing some friars who threatened to quit their posts and return to Mexico, and by threatening others, Father Ordóñez soon solidified his position and gained the complete mastery over ecclesiastical affairs which he coveted. In reality he was aiming at becoming master of all New Mexico through the subordination of even the civil authorities to his whims. This plan, of course, quickly brought him into conflict with Governor Pedro de Peralta in Santa Fe, who had no intention of suffering a diminution of either his authority or prestige. Before many weeks had passed, the two men were locked in hot debate over a string of seemingly minor issues and as tempers flared, open violence appeared imminent.

An early incident that served to strain relations between the governor and the Commissary occurred over the use of Indian labor. Peralta in drafting Pueblo Indians to work on public buildings in Santa Fe was careless in seeing that they were fed properly or that they received compensation for their labor. Ordóñez took it upon himself to intercede on behalf of the Indians and did so in such a tactless manner that the Governor's ire was greatly aroused. It is clear that the prelate's real concern was not the welfare of the Pueblo workers, but rather he saw in this issue an excellent opportunity to force the civil head to knuckle under to the Church.

Further friction developed in mid-May, 1613. A detachment of soldiers sent to Taos on official business by Governor Peralta happened to meet Fr. Ordóñez, who was on a tour of inspection at Nambé Pueblo. The Commisssary rather preemptorily ordered the men to return to Santa Fe to celebrate Mass on the feast of Pentecost which was approaching. When they reached the capital and the Governor learned what had happened, he immediately set the troops back on the road to Taos with instructions to hear Mass on the day of Pentecost at one of the Pueblo missions along the way.

Upon arriving in Santa Fe, Father Ordóñez threatened Peralta with dire consequences if he did not recall the soldiers, who by now must have been somewhat wearied of marching to and fro on the Taos road. Peralta of course indignantly refused, so the Commissary pronounced him excommunicate and nailed a formal declaration to that effect on the door of the parish church. Before leaving for his residence at Santo Domingo, Ordóñez gave careful instructions to Fr. Luís Tirado, chief priest of the villa, as to the manner in which the Governor might have the sentence of excommunication lifted. To be absolved he would have to pay a fine of fifty pesos and appear at Mass barefoot and carrying a candle, and there swear obedience to the ecclesiastical authorities. On the following Sunday, Father Tirado took another step in announcing that any citizen who so much as spoke to the Governor or removed his hat in his presence should also incur the penalty of excommunication. Stern measures these!

Father Tirado and the Governor hurled charges and countercharges at one another, in the course of which the priest issued a second decree of excommunication — perhaps on the theory that twice excommunicate, twice damned. An innocent bystander caught up in the affair was the royal notary who served Governor Peralta. Father Tirado commanded this man to cease assisting the Governor, and when the fellow complied, Peralta arrested him and sentenced him to death by strangulation. Enraged by this action, Tirado went before a meeting of the Santa Fe town council and demanded that the members of that body go at once to free the notary and while about it kill the Governor. He further declared that if they had no stomach for such business, he would take it upon himself to sally forth to do the releasing and assassinating, and if he should fail in his objectives, he would close up the church in Santa Fe and depart for Santo Domingo.

The weak-kneed councilmen, the first of a long tradition, were panic stricken and they hastened to the office of the Governor and begged him to release the notary and avoid bloodshed. Peralta agreed at once, not out of fear, he explained, but from a desire to avert disaster. Even with this temperance an explosion seemed near, particularly as the crusty Fr. Ordóñez hastened up from Santo Domingo issuing incendiary pronouncements. He threatened, for example, to round up his army of friars, march on Santa Fe and seize the Governor. Before any such seditious act could be undertaken, however, third parties intervened and worked out a shaky compromise. The public penance in the formula of absolution was omitted and the Governor agreed to return to the Church's fold. Also each side agreed to desist from exchanges of dirty names.

In spite of this truce, the bitterness ran too deep for either party to erase the scars of hatred and before long both the Governor and the clergy were back at each others' throats. One Sunday morning early in July, Governor Peralta wended his way to church, as he was now readmitted to the sacraments and was thus entitled to the dubious privilege of receiving spiritual consolation from his archenemies. Upon arriving, the

Governor was almost overcome with shock at the sight that met his eyes. His chair, his favorite chair, which usually sat in a place of honor at the front of the church, had been tossed into the street, under orders of Father Tirado someone whispered, and there it resided, up-turned, amidst the dust and burro droppings.

Choking back his choler, the Governor directed an attendant to retrieve the besmirched throne and to carry it back into the church placing it at the rear near the baptismal font and among the Indians. By this gesture, Peralta, doubtless, was expressing his preference for a seat among the unwashed to one near the high altar where the town's notables clustered.

The Governor now determined upon revenge. Later the same week when he learned that Ordóñez had arrived in Santa Fe with the intention of calling for his arrest, he gathered some of his soldiers and marched to the residence of the friars where he called out his adversaries and began to harangue them. Among other things, he loudly commanded Father Ordóñez to get out of town. More heated words followed and before anyone knew what had happened, the Governor had his pistol out and was banging away! The Commissary escaped unscathed, but not so a lay brother, Fr. Jerónimo de Pedraza, who fell wounded before the fusillade along with the royal armorer, an innocent observer of the fray. Perhaps needless to point out, ere the sun set that day, Governor Peralta had been excommunicated again. Such was the nature of passionate feuding in old Santa Fe.

As a postscript to this strange story, it must be stated that Peralta's shoot-out was his last act of defiance against the Church. Hereafter, Father Ordóñez was to have things very much his own way. During the second week in August following the shooting disturbance in Santa Fe, the Commissary received word through his spies that the Governor had left the capital and was journeying down the Camino Real on his way to Mexico City where he hoped to lodge charges against members of the clerical faction. Realizing that some of his recent acts might not seem justified under close scrutiny, Ordóñez determined to halt Peralta's trip. To this end, he sent urgent messages to the friars under him with instructions to arm themselves and report to Santo Domingo as soon as possible. Although a few responded to this unusual call, most of the padres demurred, finding various reasons to excuse their non-compliance. With his private little army, which included a group of soldiers won over to the Church's cause, Ordóñez in the dead of night descended upon Peralta's camp near Isleta, arrested the Governor in the name of the Inquisition, and imprisoned him in a small cell at Sandia mission.

What sufferings the defeated Peralta underwent during his succeeding months of captivity can only be guessed. At one point, he managed to escape, fleeing to Santa Fe where he hoped to find a few loyal partisans who would give him shelter. Unfortunately, his enemies seized him once again and although the harried official was emaciated from lack of food, he was immediately fettered, placed upon a horse, and with only an animal skin to protect his body from the piercing winter winds, was returned to confinement.

During the time Governor Peralta was held under ecclesiastical arrest, Commissary Ordóñez was virtual ruler of New Mexico, dictating orders and dispensing justice. The central government in Mexico City was so remote from affairs on the frontier that it had little or no awareness of the conditions prevailing in this far province. When a new governor arrived in Santa Fe in 1614, he quickly fell under the guiling spell of Ordóñez, and ex-Governor Peralta was only permitted to depart after suffering further humiliations and being stripped of all his property.

As unusual as all these events may appear, such violent struggle between representatives of Church and State were fairly typical of provincial life in seventeenth century New Mexico. During the administration of Governor Luís de Rosas (1637-1641), the mayhem exceeded even that of the Peralta-Ordóñez era. In one instance, the haughty Rosas accosted two friars at the chapel of San Miguel (today known popularly as "the oldest church") and there, after giving them a tongue lashing for opposing some of his immoral conduct, he commenced to budgeon them with a stick. Both of the padres were soon "bathed in blood" and as the Governor flailed away, finally breaking his stick over the head of one, he shouted curses and reviled them as liars, pigs, traitors, heretics, and schismatics. The churchmen were then placed under arrest and held in the Governor's Palace where they were threatened with execution. Both were soon released, however, and were expelled from the villa in a most battered and baleful condition.

Luís de Rosas subsequently paid for his mischief when a husband, whose wife had been tampered with, burst into his room and dispatched him with a dozen sword thrusts. As he had died excommunicate, Rosas was denied burial by the Church in consecrated ground, and hence his remains had to be laid to rest in a vacant lot.

Such incidents as these did irreparable damage to the social and political fabric of the colony. With the chief authorities engaged in fratricidal conflict, the common citizenry found it most impossible to avoid involvement. Even more troubled were the Pueblo Indians whose confusion grew as they witnessed their conquerors reducing themselves to the level of fighting animals. Under such conditions, it was exceedingly difficult to instill respect for European civilization and religion in the hearts of the native people.

From a historical view, the civil conflict was unfortunate in that it served to obscure positive aspects of life in Spanish New Mexico. Many brave settlers and heroic friars conducted themselves in a most honorable fashion and should have been remembered for their contribution to Spain's pioneering achievements on the northern frontier. Instead, their honest accomplishments often have been forgotten, while the spectacular and violent feuds promoted by a handful of unworthy individuals and recorded by their contemporaries, remain to stir the wonder of the modern reader.

OF LOVE-POTIONS AND WITCHCRAFT

Throughout the ages man has felt the presence of malevolent spirits and supernatural beings from whose evil influence he found protection in the use of magical rites. Even the most Christian Spaniards who came to the New World firmly believed in the physical presence of the Devil, in the power of witches, and in the efficacy of black magic. Provincial society in seventeenth century Santa Fe, almost completely devoid, as it was, of comforts and the usual refinements of civilization, proved a fertile ground for the growth of the lore of demonology and witchcraft. Even the most exalted pillars of the community resorted to magic on occasion. In one instance, the Spanish governor engaged an Indian woman from San Juan Pueblo who was versed in the black arts, and had her brought to Santa Fe in an effort to save the life of a soldier who had been bewitched!

In the early 1630's, a representative of the Inquisition began looking into superstitious practices of Santa Fe residents. In no time at all he collected fifty sworn statements which provided ample evidence of the lamentable state of affairs in the captial. One series of declarations concerned the soldiers, many of whom were notoriously unfaithful to their wives. In such a small town, no man could hope to keep his indiscretions secret for long, and where other news was scarce, the news-hungry fed themselves on the sordid gossip which concerned their neighbor's private doings. The investigation into this matter revealed that the aggrieved wives, in a desperate bid to recover the affection and loyalty of their husbands, were trafficking in love-potions and other devices of an occult nature. Most of the mixtures and formulas being handed about and slipped into breakfast cups seem to have originated with the Mexican Indian servants attached to the majority of households. Their recipes included the use of herbs, powders, cornmeal, milk, worms — fried or mashed — and urine, either of the husband or his mistress. The purpose of concoctions constructed from such ingredients was to win back the man's devotion, or at the very least make him lose interest in his outside love. Although the women, in resorting to these supernatural artifices, were risking censure by the Church and the Inquisition, they evidently persevered with their potions in hopes of succeeding where feminine wiles had failed and restoring true love to the family hearth.

A more serious situation that became apparent at this time concerned a mother and daughter against whom charges of sorcery were leveled. The unfortunate creatures were Beatriz de los Angeles, a Mexican Indian, and Juana de la Cruz, her child born of a Spanish father. Both were well-known dispatchers of herbal potions, and around each had collected a trove of stories regarding past successes at hexing and bewitching people. Beatriz, it was widely believed, had attempted to perfect her diabolical powers by experimenting on two native servants, both of whom had sickened and died. Following this, she had sought revenge on her lover because he beat her, and she gave him a specially prepared drink that produced agonizing stomach pains and eventually caused his death. And others, it was said, had suffered a like fate because they incurred the anger of this devilish woman.

The daughter, Juana, was believed guilty of similar crimes. Just as her mother had done, she was reported to have killed a cruel lover by bewitching him. Juana possessed the evil eye and had hexed several children merely by handling and looking at them. Even more bizarre was the widely-repeated tale that she was capable of long flights over vast distances, her aim being on such excursions to spy on her many paramours and observe if they were faithful. Unlike traditional witches, Juana scorned the flying broom; her journeys were made inside an egg!

Although these and other fabrications were presented to an official of the Inquisition in Santa Fe, there is no indication that he took them seriously. Witchcraft stories were always plentiful and they exercised a strong hold on the popular mind. Under the circumstances it was quite easy for simpleminded folk to assign all manner of strange meanings to any form of deviant behavior observed in their neighbor's yard. And what better way to avenge yourself of some slight than to brand your enemy as a witch or sorcerer.

Signature of Antonio de Otermin.

RECKONING IN BLOOD

It was late in the afternoon of August 9, 1680, the eve of the feast of San Lorenzo, when two Pueblo Indians crossed the bare plaza in Santa Fe and entered the reception room in the casa real. In halting Spanish they explained to an orderly that they bore urgent news which required an immediate audience with Governor Antonio de Otermín. Ushered into the Governor's presence, the two men identified themselves as officers of Pecos and Tanos Pueblos. Professing to be sincere friends and brothers of the Spaniards, they told of a secret plot that had been hatched by certain Indians who were hoping to foment an open rebellion. The conspirators were centered in the Pueblos north of Santa Fe, but they had drawn into their net most of the other villages of the province. Their aim was simple — to exterminate all Spaniards in New Mexico.

The informants stated that they had been approached by two Tesuque Indians who attempted to lure them into the conspiracy, but they had refused being unwilling to participate in such wickedness and treason. Instead, the pair had hastened to Santa Fe to make their report and declare their loyalty. Otermín listened gravely, then thanked the Indians for giving notice and bade them return to their homes and remain quiet.

The distress of New Mexico's governor at this moment can be easily imagined. He had known for some time that the Pueblos were restive — they had never fully accepted the heavy burden of the Spanish yoke — but he had felt content that the power of the colonists' arms could prevail over any disturbance. Otermín, nevertheless, was a cautious man, so he dispatched messengers to the outlying missions and to the settlers concentrated in the down river district south of Santa Fe warning them to be on guard.

After a fitfull night's sleep, the Governor aroused himself and started for church to hear Mass. Before he reached his destination, however, a sudden commotion in the plaza arrested his attention. A priest had dashed into town with the calamitous news that the Tesuque Indians had risen that morning, slain Father Pio, desecrated their chruch, and fled to the mountains taking all the livestock belonging to the mission. Instantly a wail went up and the entire villa was thrown into the greatest turmoil. The Governor quickly assembled a squadron of soldiers and sent it out to ascertain the gravity of the situation. When the men returned, ashen-faced, they reported the entire northern district was in flames. Churches had been profaned, priests murdered, haciendas burned, and men, women, and children killed, their bodies left strewn along the road. The great rebellion had begun!

The full gravity of the disaster became known as refugees began pouring into Santa Fe from all quarters. Repeated attempts to establish contact with settlers in the far south proved futile. Governor Otermín arranged for all the people in the villa to retire to the complex of structures that constituted the casas reales or government buildings, believing these to be most defensible. As the days passed, new stories trickled in concerning the terror in the countryside and the mounting fury of the Indians, who were greatly inspired by their victories.

Early one morning the vanguard of the native armies made its appearance in the southern suburb of the captial. With war-whoops and loud cries they began igniting the cornfields and scattered homes located there, and shortly they fired the chapel of San Miguel. One of the rebel leaders, conversant in Spanish, came forward under a flag of truce to confer with the Governor. He carried two banners, one red and the other white, and he announced that the Spaniards should choose between them: if they selected the white they would be permitted to leave the country in peace, but if they settled on the red and continued to resist, all would perish since the rebels were numerous and their ranks were swelling hourly.

Otermín upbraided the emissary for the crimes which had already been committed and promised swift punishment if the pillaging on the outskirts of the city did not cease. The Indian returned to his camp to be greeted by peals of bells and trumpets and wild shouts from his comrades. It would be a war to the finish.

The Spanish Governor was aware that only the most resolute

resistance would save his people from utter annihilation. Accordingly, he called out all his soldiers, few though they were, and ordered an assault on the rebel position. The men crossed the river and fell upon the Indians, who took shelter in the ruins of San Miguel chapel and nearby houses. But at that point reenforcements from the Tewa Pueblos appeared on the northern perimeter of the villa and the troops found themselves obliged to retreat to the main plaza and prepare for its defense.

That night the Indians camped in the foothills east of town, the yellow pinpoints of their fires clearly visible to the weary soldiers who kept watch from the roof of the Governor's Palace. At dawn they poured down out of the heights, but pulled up short when they observed the Spaniards coming to meet them in full battle array with Governor Otermín in the lead. This fearless show of force caused the Indians to withdraw to the hills again and to await the arrival of still more warriors from some of the remoter pueblos. The bravado of the Spaniards had staved off an attack for the moment, but the situation remained critical. On succeeding days, Indians began moving in toward the center of town sacking and burning buildings and entrenching themselves in new positions. Finally, having assembled nearly 2,500 fighting men, they pulled the noose so tight the Spaniards were confined to the casas reales with the water supply cut off and no hope of aid from the outside. Some of the boldest attackers managed to charge the tower door on the eastern end of the Palace, where they attempted to kindle a fire, but were driven back with severe losses. In his journal Otermín wrote, "We passed this night, like the rest, with much care and watchfulness, and suffered greatly from thirst because of the scarcity of water."

And yet the worst was still to come. As the foe took possession of portions of the plaza, the church and other prominent buildings were put to the torch. Throughout the night the flames raged and a great pall of smoke hung over the city. By the light of the conflagration, the jubilant Indians danced, paraded, sang, and held up for ridicule many of the sacred articles that had been plundered from the churches. And they filled the night air with victory chants and recited litanies of wrongs suffered at the hands of the Spaniards.

Inside the Governor's Palace and casas reales the moans of wounded soldiers mingled with the wails of women and children and were carried over the walls by a gentle summer breeze to merge outside with the din of Indian drumming and chanting. There had been no water for two days and the food was all but gone. The beleaguered Spaniards had bestirred themselves to a heroic defense, but now their cause seemed lost. In anguish, Governor Otermín summoned his men and in a moving speech expressed his intention of going out to meet the enemy face to face and either dying or conquering.

On the following morning a special Mass was celebrated and each soldier commended himself to the Almighty. Then the gates were thrown open and mounted or on foot, every man rushed into the plaza with a lusty shout. The Indians were taken unaware by this sudden maneuver and although resisting courageously, they slowly gave ground. The Spaniards fought like angry panthers with their backs to the wall, and the ferocity of their charge carried them all the way to the banks of the river where at last they could slake their thrist. Otermín, his torso covered with blood from a chest wound, regrouped his troops and swung them out on the east flank toward the eminence known now as Marcy Hill. Here the foe was most heavily concentrated and the Spaniards surrounded several houses where the Indians had lodged themselves and from which they were now firing with bows and arrows and captured arquebuses. The structures were set afire and as warriors scurried out like startled quail, they were cut down by a barrage of bullets. According to the Spaniards, they slew more than 300 Indians in this one encounter.

Governor Otermín, who had received two more arrow wounds in the face, commanded his men to fall back on the plaza which at last remained clear of the enemy. Although the Spaniards now had water, their condition remained perilous since the Pueblos were reforming their armies and calling for renewed support from their allies. As a result, the fateful decision to abandon the capital was made, and on Monday, the 19th of August of 1680, the survivors marched out in good order "without a crust of bread or a grain of wheat" for provisions, although they did have a small herd of livestock which had been saved. Thus the siege of Santa Fe was ended, representing one of the worst defeats ever suffered by Spain in her New World empire.

Governor Antonio de Otermín and his fugitive train escaped and New Mexico, for all practical purposes, was surrendered to the Pueblo Indians. True, a kind of government in exile was established at El Paso del Norte (present Cd. Juarez), but all control over the upper Rio Grande valley was lost.

In the following year, 1681, Otermín was turned back by the

Pueblos in an abortive attempt to reclaim the province, and shortly afterward he was replaced by a new governor at El Paso. The reconquest of New Mexico, in fact, had to wait almost a dozen years until the Spaniards on the northern frontier could marshal their strength and until the rebellious Indians had become disorganized through internal quarrels.

General Diego de Vargas, an aristocratic and able soldier, was named to the governorship in 1691 with precise instructions to subdue the Indians and restore Spain's flag over the territory abandoned a decade before. In the two years which followed, he campaigned relentlessly, bringing the Pueblo people under control by a policy which exhibited leniency for those who submitted and stern punishment for any who remained unreconciled. In the ruined capital of Santa Fe, De Vargas' army discovered that many Indians had occupied the old buildings left by the Spaniards at the time of the revolt and had remodeled them to conform to their own architectural requirements. When it was made clear the native people would have to vacate their homes and leave the city once again to the Spaniards, they became belligerent and De Vargas was required to dislodge them by force. Several leaders of the Indians taken in this fray were hanged on the plaza, and De Vargas raised aloft over the Governor's Palace the same banner used by Oñate almost a century before.

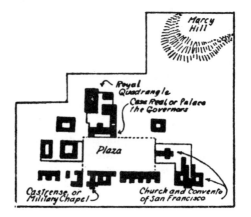

Plan of the old Santa Fe plaza.

THE FIRST URBAN RENEWAL

Don Juan Bautista de Anza was appointed governor of New Mexico in 1777, serving two terms until his retirement in 1789. As one of the ablest as well as most amiable men who ever occupied that office, Anza is perhaps best remembered for the decisive defeat which he inflicted upon the warlike Comanches. His skill as a fighter and diplomat eventually enabled him to pacify these troublesome Indians and bring them into a close alliance with the Spaniards. Moreover, he succeeded in dissolving the traditional friendship between the Apaches and Navajos, turning those tribes against one another and diverting their hostile activities away from the colonial settlements.

One interesting and rather curious aspect of Anza's governorship concerned his plans for the reorganization of the town of Santa Fe. Upon assuming office, he had been given instructions by his superiors in Mexico to survey the towns and villages of the province with an eye to improving their defenses. Officials for some time had been critical of he way the New Mexicans scattered over the countryside, stringing their houses and farms in random fashion along streams and irrigation ditches so that even the larger communities were highly vulnerable to Indian attack. The colonists for convenience preferred to be located near their fields, but for their own protection it was decreed that they should congregate in compact and well-regulated settlements.

With some degree of success Governor Anza managed to concentrate the people in the Albuquerque district, who had been spread for several leagues along the Rio Grande, and those living in the Santa Cruz valley. When it came to Santa Fe, however, a major problem arose, for Anza found the citizens here stubbornly opposed to the urban renewal program which he had devised.

At this time, New Mexico's capital had a population of not much more than 2,000, but because of the dispersal of the population for a considerable distance up and down the Santa Fe river, the limits of the town had been stretched to three leagues, or about 7.5 miles. At this period, too, regular, well-maintained streets were practically non-existent, even in the areas near the plaza. Instead, lanes or mere paths gave access to the scattered houses, while cornfields and orchards could be found in the very center of the community.

Anza's predecessor, Governor Fermín de Mendinueta, had given some thought to correcting this situation, but he had acknowledged that any attempt at municipal reform would be opposed by Santa Fe residents, who were of a "churlish nature" and were not willing to give up "the perfect freedom in which they had always lived." Fully cognizant that he would have to deal with the displeasure of the local citizens, Anza reviewed the condition of the town, prepared a feasibility study, and submitted a renewal program for approval to his military superior, the commandant general whose headquarters was in Arizpe, Sonora.

According to the plan, the old plaza would be abandoned, government buildings razed, and the villa re-formed in a compact manner in the Barrio de Analco on the south side of the river. The Christianized Indians (called *genízaros*) who lived in Analco would be moved to a new town founded for them out on the frontier. The presidio or military garrison would not remain in the capital, but would be transferred to a new location on the Rio Grande, midway between Cochití and Santo Domingo Pueblos.

It may be that Anza chose to move the center of town to the Analco suburb, because that site was on higher ground and hence less subject to flooding. In any case, his proposals were approved, and some initial steps were taken to put the program into effect. For example, the officers and men of the Santa Fe garrison voluntarily contributed 2,175 pesos toward the cost of establishing the new military installation. Before matters could proceed much further, however, the disgruntled residents of Santa Fe took action to halt the project.

Although no documentary record of it has come to light, we may be sure that from the beginning Anza's activities were challenged by his subjects. No doubt, formal petitions and protests were delivered to him, but from all indications he chose to ignore them. As a last resort, twenty-four members of the community announced their intention of leaving the province to make an appeal to higher authority in Mexico. Governor Anza indignantly refused them travel permits and indicated they would be restrained by force if necessary. Notwithstandng, the men escaped in secret and fled south to Arizpe. There, in an interview with the commandant general, they presented their case so forcefully that an order was won forbidding the Governor of New Mexico from moving the villa of Santa Fe and from transferring the Indians or *genízaros* of Analco to the frontier until the entire matter could be reviewed. Furthermore, the commandant general decreed that, henceforward, citizens had the right to leave the province without interference when they wished to make an appeal to the superior government.

From the contemporary records it is not difficult to reconstruct the arguments that the Santa Feans must have presented in support of the plea to suspend reorganization of their town. Concentration of the people in a new and easily-defensible plaza as projected by the Governor would, doubtless, have provided greater security, but this would have been offset somewhat by the removal of the *genízaros*, who were excellent fighters and helped protect the capital. More significantly, under the new arrangement citizens would be obliged to live apart from their fields, thus leaving their crops prey to thieves and wild animals. Bears ranging down out of the foothills of the Sangre de Cristos were especially destructive, and unattended cornfields could be devastated in the course of an hour. Certainly, they thought, it was more important to guard the food supply, even at the risk of exposing one's family to Indian raids.

The restraining order issued by the commandant general, as subsequent events proved, meant total defeat for Anza's ambitious plan to reorganize Santa Fe. In the end, the plaza remained on its original site as did the old military presidio, which within several years was completely rebuilt. Had Governor Anza's work been carried out, the colonial capital would have been placed in better order and greater safety extended to its inhabitants. But whatever their own motives, we can be grateful to those Santa Feans who risked the journey to Sonora, since the net effect of their resistance to regimentation and municipal reorganization was that the historic Governor's Palace and other fine residences were preserved for the enjoyment of later generations. That was a result, of course, which probably was forseen by no one at the time.

A REMARKABLE CELEBRATION

It was early February in Santa Fe with the air crisp and cold and the peaks above the city laden with snow. In the house of the chief alcalde, a group of town notables had assembled for the purpose of planning an independence day celebration. Many hastily contrived suggestions and recommendations were laid on the table, and much earnest discussion ensued as to the proper manner of procedure in such cases. But truthfully, no one among these leading pillars of the community had the slightest notion where to begin. For more than two centuries the New Mexicans had been subjects of the king of Spain and suddenly to find themselves part of the independent nation of Mexico left them quite bewildered. The formal separation had occurred the previous summer, 1821, with the signing of the Treaty of Córdova far to the south, but with the slowness of communication and the uncertainty of conditions in Mexico City, this select council of Santa Feans was only now convening to take up the matter of celebrating the change in political fortunes.

When the distinguished gentlemen finally reached an impasse in their deliberations, someone suggested that authoritative advice be sought. And who could offer better counsel than a citizen of the United States, a nation independent now almost fifty years. Certainly a representative of the United States could tell them what to do. Accordingly, a summons went forth to Mr. Thomas James, a merchant recently arrived in Santa Fe, and when he appeared before the alcalde's gathering, the nature of the problem was explained.

"Señor James, what is the custom in your country on such occasions? Give us your advice," And Señor James obliged.

"I suggest you raise a liberty pole," he said. "Send men into the

32

mountains for the tallest pine that can be found and erect it in the plaza. Then you should run up a flag, a new flag honoring your nation. And you ought to fire a salute for each of Mexico's provinces. How many provinces are there anyway?"

Nobody seemed to know. Voices buzzed. Fingers were counted and lines marked on paper. When the provinces or states were totalled, it was discovered that Mexico had twenty-one, counting Texas. Madre de Dios, this was serious and difficult business — organizing a celebration.

Surely the *simpático* Señor James would not mind assuming complete charge, he was so wise in these matters. Thus to the great relief of the alcalde and his associates, Mr. James, late of St. Louis, agreed to superintend independence day festivities in Santa Fe.

That an Anglo-American was entrusted with such a task, in itself offers evidence that a new attitude prevailed in New Mexico. During the last twenty-five years of Spanish rule, officials in Santa Fe had demonstrated considerable concern over United States pressure along New Mexico's ill-defined northern and eastern boundary. In 1807 young Lieutenant Zebulon Pike with a handful of men had thrown up a small stockade near the upper Rio Grande and had promptly been arrested by a hundred soldiers from Santa Fe. Taken to New Mexico's capital under guard, Pike was singularly unimpressed by the town's appearance, describing the adobe houses from a distance as resembling flat bottomed boats on the Ohio River. After many days of interrogation, he was sent to Chihuahua, then subsequently permitted to return home, carrying the warning that Americans were unwelcome in New Mexico. Nevertheless, a number of traders and trappers entered the province in the years after 1810, and inevitably they were roughly handled by the authorities. The citizens, however, desired commercial contact with their eastern neighbors, and as soon as the heavy hand of Spain had been lifted, New Mexico opened her doors and welcomed merchants and businessmen from the United States. Thomas James, one of the first to take advantage of the new hospitality, reached Santa Fe with a supply of merchandise on the first day of December, 1821, rented a building for a store, and was soon doing a thriving business.

Several days after the meeting in the alcalde's house, a wood party was formed under James' direction and was sent into the neighboring mountains to obtain a suitable pine for a flagpole. The men returned with a trunk thirty feet long, but this was deemed inadequate, so they were sent out again. Another tree much longer than the first was secured, and the two were spliced together, a flag rope was attached, and the whole was raised as a liberty pole to a height of almost seventy feet. Still the problem remained of a suitable emblem, since the New Mexicans were unsure if a flag for the new nation had been adopted. This difficulty resolved itself when it was decided to create a special banner appropriate for the occasion — James, for obvious reasons, recommended an eagle, but officials finally agreed upon two clasped hands representing friendship toward all men and nations. With these preparations complete, Thomas James retired to his quarters.

Early on the morning of February 5, he was aroused by a messenger from the governor, requesting his immediate presence at the plaza. Hurriedly throwing on this clothes, James proceeded to the square where all was in confusion. A dozen prominent citizens were grouped around Governor Facundo Melgares, everyone in a quandary. As James approached, all eyes turned to him expectantly.

"Very simple," he announced. "Everything is ready for raising the flag. And that honor, of course, belongs to His Excellency, the Governor."

"Oh, do it yourself, Señor James. You understand such things." And in this casual manner, Governor Melgares directed an American citizen to raise the first flag over the independent state of New Mexico.

So up went the flag, a cannon boomed shattering the early morning quiet, and Santa Feans from all quarters of the city came running toward the plaza, many of them only half-dressed and perhaps, from the noise, fearing an Indian attack. When it became clear the cannon signaled the opening of a grand fiesta, alarm changed to merriment and in the words of James, "One universal jubilee, like bedlam broke loose, reigned in Santa Fe for five days and nights. During this whole time, the city exhibited a scene of universal carousing and revelry; . . . and thus did these rejoicing republicans continue the celebration of their Independence."

34

THE EARLIEST MUNICIPAL CODE

In 1833 a set of municipal ordinances relating to public health and good government was proclaimed in Santa Fe. It was probably the first such formal measure taken by any city in the Southwest.

The architect of the ordinances was Don Antonio Barreiro, a native of Mexico, who had been sent by the central government in 1831 to serve as *asesor*, or official legal adviser, for the territory. At this date New Mexico still formed one of the northern provinces of the Republic of Mexico.

During his residence in Santa Fe, Barreiro became numbered among the town's prominent citizens. In his own words, he "soon came to love with devoted ardor" his new home. But he also clearly saw its many imperfections. This is evident in some of the ordinances relating to public health and welfare which he drew up and issued in 1833. Several of them have a decided modern ring.

One section, for example, pertains to public cleanliness. "For the good of the city, stagnant pools or putrid ponds must be drained. Also, irrigation ditches and streams must be kept cleaned and persons prevented from polluting or befouling them with garbage, dead animals, or whatever else. And streets and plazas must be tidied, always swept and dampened in the summer."

At a time when pollution from mechanical engines was still a century or more away, the forward-looking Barreiro was already concerned with preserving New Mexico's pure air. One of his laws read: "Everyone is forbidden from burning garbage, rags, or anything else, either in his fireplace or outside, which may cause an offensive odor, except when, in the judgment of the civil magistrates, it becomes necessary to destroy trash piles that now exist."

Another of his ordinances covered the regulation of cemeteries. "Care must be exercised to see that graves will be at least two and half yards in depth. Cemeteries must be placed down wind from regular air currents which blow through the town. Further, it is forbidden that cadavers remain unburied for more than 24 hours. An exception will be made with bodies delivered over from hanging which can be buried later, so that officials can make certain that they are really dead."

Long before the Food and Drug Administration had been thought of in the United States, Antonio Barreiro was setting standards for food consumed by Santa Fe residents. He decreed that all meats must be healthful and of good quality, and he sternly forbade anyone from selling meat from animals which had died of rabies. Town officials were to be designated whose duty was to inspect the cleanliness of flours and grains and remove from public sale all unsanitary products and green and rotten fruit.

One curious provision of the ordinances governed the activities of midwives, important people in the days when doctors were scarce. They were not allowed to deliver babies without a license granted by a municipal judge and without a certificate from their parish priest proving that they knew how to administer baptism.

Barreiro also slipped in a statement requiring creation of a public health bureau which, among other duties, would obtain and dispense smallpox vaccine. Since no reference can be found to such a bureau in later documents, we can assume that it was never formed.

The municipal measures of 1833 included a safety code designed to protect the population from accidents. Residents were warned not to throw garbage and dirty water out their doors and into the streets, lest they hit passersby. Horsemen could not race their mounts in the streets, and they were instructed to keep their pack animals from running over old folks and children. Another injunction prohibited tying animals to posts holding up porches. Evidently, some unruly mule had pulled down a porch roof or two on the heads of innocent victims.

If we can believe the reports of Missouri traders who visited Santa Fe about this time, the local people were much dedicated to public dances and balls. Sometimes these functions got out of hand, so the ordinances decreed: "All dances require permission of a judge who will set conditions and prohibit those dances in houses where suspicion exists that a disturbance or a threat to public morals may develop."

Finally, the sensible author of the municipal ordinances saw the need to protect the serenity of Santa Fe from the inroads of noise pollution. His laws banned the shooting of firearms inside the city limits, and declared further: "Shouts, yells, and other outside demonstrations are prohibited, especially those which may scandalize or disturb public order in the silence of the night."

Don Antonio Barrerio — literate, cultivated, and public-spirited — seems to have been something of an environmentalist, a man ahead of his time.

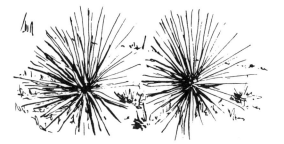

A GOVERNOR LOSES HIS HEAD

On Agua Fria Street in a western suburb of Santa Fe, a small boulder with a polished face and inscription until recently lay enclosed within a rusting iron fence. The words carved in stone read:

Governor Pérez was assasinated on
this spot, Aug. 9, 1837

This inconspicuous monument served as a reminder of a most tragic and bloody event which occurred in the time when New Mexico owed allegiance to the Mexican Republic.*

Albino Pérez had been a colonel in the Mexican army when he was appointed by President Santa Anna to become governor of this distant province. Pérez came to his new position with high hopes. The region of his government, he knew, was poor and backward as compared to the more developed portions of the country in the south, but with work and vision, the situation could be improved, and under intelligent leadership New Mexico made to contribute her share to the nation. Unfortunately, Pérez was young and brassy and had an aristrocratic manner which failed to win the approval of the rustic New Mexicans. In fact, he came to be regarded as an alien and an outsider and though he married a Santa Fe woman, he remained aloof from social affairs.

At the very time Pérez assumed his governorship, the central government in Mexico City was in the process of reducing powers of the provinces and concentrating authority at the national capital. This did not sit well with hardy individualists on the frontier who resented any interference in local affairs, and in New Mexico Governor Pérez was viewed

* The boulder has now been moved to the courtyard of the Governor's Palace.

as an agent of centralist forces bent upon extinguishing the last vestige of local autonomy. When a direct tax was levied on all forms of business, many New Mexicans grumbled loudly and swore the national government intended to bleed them dry.

Finally in the summer of 1837, dissatisfaction with the rule of Albino Pérez and with policies he was charged to enforce resulted in an insurrection, popularly called the Chimayó Rebellion. Rebel forces made up of poor folk and Pueblo Indians collected in the Chimayó Valley and prepared to resist an army from Santa Fe led by the Governor. The troops of Pérez were composed mostly of "volunteers" who had been pressed into service, and as soon as the enemy appeared the government ranks dissolved, leaving the commander alone with a few followers. Fleeing toward Santa Fe for his life, Governor Pérez reached the city late in the evening, and there, after sending his wife and small child into hiding, he set out with several trusted friends toward the south.

As the hour was late, the party halted to spend the night at the ranch of El Alamo, a few miles below the capital. On the following morning, a band of Pueblo Indians attacked the ranch, and everyone scattered to save himself as best he could. Governor Pérez fled on foot back toward Santa Fe, but was overtaken on the main highway, the old Camino Real, only one league from the plaza. According to reports he put up a desperate defense, but was swiftly felled by an arrow in the breast. Even while the heart still beat, his assailants severed the head from his body and carried it about on the end of a lance as a trophy. Shouting and singing, the victors paraded to the main rebel camp on the north edge of town near Rosario Church and there the late governor's head was tossed upon a field and kicked about in a game of football. Other civil officers were also slain on the same day, and shortly the rebel army from the north entered Santa Fe in triumph and installed as governor one of its own members, José González of Taos.

Many honest citizens were thoroughly frightened by the political upheaval, and no matter how they may have disapproved of Albino Pérez, they could not countenance the barbaric manner in which he had met his end. Most Santa Feans locked their doors and prepared to await the outcome of these turbulent events.

Opposition to the new rebel regime was not long in materializing. In the area around Albuquerque, a force of loyal citizens was mustered into an army and with a former governor, Manuel Armijo, in command, it marched on Santa Fe where the insurrectionists were defeated and dispersed in a series of skirmishes. Four of the rebel leaders were executed by firing squad at the site of La Garita, a small hill just north of the present Bank of Santa Fe. The deposed governor, José González, led before Manuel Armijo, greeted his conquerer cordially and with every sign of respect. Armijo returned the courtesy, then declared, "Confess yourself, my friend, for I'm going to have you shot." And he did.

A CROOKED DERBY

For days no one in Santa Fe had talked of anything but the impending horse race. New Mexicans were inveterate gamblers and in quieter moments contented themselves with betting at monte tables or Sunday afternoon cockfights. But a good horse race was sure to stir the blood and bring forth wagers of staggering sums.

The details of this particular contest were well known. Manuel Armijo, governor since the Chimayó Rebellion two years previously, had fallen to arguing with one of his young kinsmen over which possessed the fastest horse. To settle the dispute, a race had been agreed upon, with each man wagering 5,000 pesos on his own entry. During the fifteen days set aside to prepare the horses, word spread throughout the territory, and people began flocking to the capital to witness the event and bet.

The person who had accepted Governor Armijo's sporting challenge was Manuel Antonio Chaves, a youth who would become one of New Mexico's most famous scouts and Indian fighters. In his early twenties at this time, Chaves was slight of build and of medium height with fair skin, high, prominent cheek bones, and chestnut hair. His delicate appearance, however, was misleading for underneath he was tempered steel.

As a mere boy he had gone with a party of fifty New Mexicans to fight the Navajos and had been the only survivor when the campaigners were surrounded near Canyon de Chelly and slaughtered by the Indians. Young Chaves had fought like a seasoned veteran until three serious wounds laid him low and he was left for dead on the battlefield. Later, recovering consciousness, he found the body of his brother, who had

41

been the expedition's leader, and after burying it in a sandy arroyo, started his slow and painful trek toward home several hundred miles to the east. Days later in the area north of the San Mateo Peaks, he was discovered by a shepherd, more dead than alive. But he recovered and grew to manhood, learning the hard lessons of the frontier. He became an expert shot with a rifle, a deadly marksman with a bow and arrow, and his superb horsemanship won him a reputation throughout New Mexico.

Precisely when Chaves took up residence in Santa Fe is not certain, but it was sometime in the later 1830's. His aristocratic bearing, his fame as a gallant fighter, and his cordial manner toward all soon won him many friends, and he was often a guest in the leading homes. Moreover, the stable of fine horses he collected became the talk of the capital.

Less popular was Governor Manuel Armijo, sometimes mentioned as Chaves' uncle, who had earned a name for shrewdness and hard dealing and whose moral imperfections were common gossip. Manual Chaves was evidently aware of the caliber of man against whom he competed, because he took the most stringent precautions to protect his horse before the well-publicized race. Each night the animal was locked in a stall and Roman Baca, a younger half brother, was enlisted to sleep inside on a pile of straw and serve as guard.

The day of the great event arrived and a crowd of spectators thronged to the race ground, a level space of land where the Indian School now stands. The length of the course marked off was one thousand yards and a rope was stretched taut to designate the finish line. It had been previously agreed that once the gun sounded, no accident would be considered in determining the outcome of the race.

Excited onlookers crowded around the track laying last minute bets, most of which were on the the Chaves horse. The young man had assured his friends they could place their money with all confidence since his animal was certain to win. Armijo in a jovial mood took all bets. Women wagered their jewels and some men their entire fortunes.

As the two horses were led to the starting post, excitement mounted. Roman Baca was riding the entry of his half brother; he had stripped the saddle and was astride bareback to give his mount every advantage. Manuel Chaves, standing near the Governor and other dignitaries at the finish, kept a sharp watch on the proceedings, determined to see that all rules were observed.

Bang! The signal was fired and a great shout burst from the crowd as the horses leaped forward. Immediately, Chaves saw his own steed take the lead, and with jockey Roman glued to his back, move far ahead with long easy strides. This was not a race but a runaway. Then, inexplicably, only fifty yards from victory, the Chaves horse faltered and suddenly fell. Young Roman leaped clear, as Armijo's animal thundered past and dashed across the line.

The spectators were stunned! The race was over and lost to the Governor. But no one moved. Chaves slowly walked out on the track as the jockey got to his feet beating the dust from his clothes. It was apparent to all that the horse was dead. But how could such a thing have happened? What strange quirk of fate could have produced this tragedy? Armijo appeared strangely unconcerned, and with a few intimate friends who had bet with him, he went among the crowd collecting a rich harvest. With people on all sides muttering that they had been betrayed, the stricken Manuel Chaves could do nothing but escape the field as quickly as possible. To lose was no dishonor, but to lose in this way and to bring misfortune on one's friends was painful to bear. And thus the great horse race was ended, although in a most unexpected manner.

But the affair was not closed. Manuel brooded for weeks, and finally made an earnest attempt to put his loss out of mind. Then, almost three months after the race he had a strange caller. The man was a Frenchman and a physician. He explained that he lived in the quarters of an American merchant, John Scolly, who maintained a store on the plaza, and that he had a dreadful confession to make.

Chaves listened, his face tense, as the story unfolded. Governor Armijo, the Frenchman explained, had come to him a short time before the horse race and had offered him 1500 pesos to arrange matters so that he would win. The work would have to be done cleverly in order that no one could suspect foul play. Whether from greed or from fear of the Governor, the physician had accepted the commission, and the night before the race had carried out the design in this fashion: going to the Chaves stable, he silently pried loose a window, and observing Roman asleep on his pallet, he passed in a sponge soaked in anesthesia and tied to the end of a long pole. After the boy had been rendered unconscious, he slipped inside and fed the horse a slow-acting poison. It was for this reason the poor beast had fallen dead on the race track next day. Armijo, the doctor wailed, had not kept his bargain. Instead of the payoff promised, he had given only 150 pesos and had threatened to shoot him if he did not depart the country immediately.

Manual sat silently throughout the tale, his rage seething within. After the terrified man had left, he reviewed the entire business in his mind and came to the conclusion that the only proper punishment for Armijo was death. Carefully going over his arrows, he selected several with smooth straight shafts, and taking up his bow, the one he used in contests with friendly Indians, he slipped out of his house and headed for the Governors Palace.

Night had long since blanketed the town and pools of black shadow lay in the lee of adobe walls. From the murky darkness alongside the Palace, Manuel surveyed the long portal which faced the open plaza. He was aware that Armijo often returned late in the evening from a clandestine rendezvous with his consort, a notorious woman-about-town who operated a gambling hall by day. If he could catch the Governor alone and if his aim was true, an arrow in the breast would furnish the vengeance he sought.

Loud voices drifted toward him and Manuel faded deeper into the shadows. Several men passed by in the street and one glanced his way. Had he been seen? No matter. They continued on. But Manuel Armijo made no appearance that night, and young Chaves returned home in the early morning hours before dawn. He fully intended to stalk his prey again that same evening, but providence intervened. Armijo had found him out and orders were soon abroad for the arrest of Manuel Chaves. Friends, however, brought him word in time, and collecting his best horses he fled the town heading east.

The Governor was furious that his nephew, Manuelito, as he called him had slipped through his fingers, and at once he set a troop of soldiers on the trail. At the same time he posted a reward of 10,000 pesos for the young man's head. Chaves, nevertheless, made good his escape, riding his horses to exhaustion and then joining a freight train bound for St. Louis. For him it would be exile in the United States, until time adjusted affairs and made it safe to return to his native country. And all this, the consequence of an argument over who had the fastest horse.

NEW BRANCHES OF THE TREE

It was August of 1846 as 1500 men marched into New Mexico singing in hearty voice:

Colonel Kearny you can bet,
Will keep the boys in motion,
Till Yankee Land includes the sand
Along the Pacific Ocean.

These jaunty soldiers formed the Army of the West, forty days out of Ft.
Leavenworth and on the road to the conquest of New Mexico and points
beyond. Their song reflected the spirit of Manifest Destiny which
enlivened the hearts of the people of the United States at this time and
drove them ever westering across the heart of the continent.

Colonel Stephen Watts Kearny (soon elevated to brigadier general)
commanded this expedition and arranged the plans for detaching New
Mexico from the Mexican Republic and adding it to the Union. His instructions from President Polk were explicit: to carry out the conquest in
as peaceful a manner as possible, conciliate the people, and effect the
change of allegiance with grace and dignity. Kearny's task was eased and
his ends accomplished when New Mexican resistance dissolved before
the surge of his army. Governor Manuel Armijo made motions of rally-
ing the people and of preparing to oppose the invading Anglo-Americans
at Apache Canyon east of Santa Fe, but New Mexico was short of war
materiel, trained soldiers were few, and the Governor's unpopularity and
lack of generalmanship rendered him unfit to lead in a moment of crisis.
So Armijo, loading what he could plunder into seven wagons, hastened
south to Durango, and left Santa Fe to receive Kearny as it chose.

As it developed, Santa Fe and most of New Mexico were more

amenable to the turn of events that might have been supposed. The area by now had closer commercial and economic ties with the United States than with Mexico, and the long presence of many Anglos in the provincial settlements had established some basis for mutual respect and toleration. Added to this, fears of oppression by the new regime were allayed by General Kearny as he raised the stars and bars over the ancient Governors Palace and proclaimed that the New Mexicans would be protected in their persons, property, and religion, and would, henceforth, enjoy all the privileges of American citizens. And although there was evidence of discontent in Santa Fe later in the year, and although a brief rebellion in Taos took the life of civil governor Charles Bent, New Mexico soon accepted her fortune and settled in to absorb and rework those alien ways which could serve her own uses.

»»»»

For all newcomers to Santa Fe in early Territorial days, the capital presented a wild and colorful face, offering the exotic aura of some foreign and mysterious land. The flat roof adobe houses, narrow picturesque streets, and open plaza were a reminder of Mediterranean scenes, while the noisy clutter of the market place suggested the bazaars of the Orient. The plaza at this time was more spacious than it is today and lacked the softening touch of trees: on the expanse of hard packed adobe ground, wagons were parked, horses and burros were tied while their owners conducted business, wood and hay were stacked for sale, and the Cavalry occasionally drilled. Around the fringes of the plaza, the country people collected to sell their meat, fruit, vegetables, bread, piñon nuts, and medicinal herbs, many sitting patiently all day waiting for a customer with scarcely a dollar's worth of merchandise before them. Indians from neighboring pueblos also participated, bringing wares on their own or donkey backs. In season venison, turkey, and perhaps bear were offered for sale, the fresh meat being hung from ropes suspended from the portal of the Governors Palace.

Contributing to the holiday air of the markets were the gaming tables conveniently placed everywhere, so that a wealthy ranchero from the countryside, a prosperous trader from St. Louis, a soldier recently paid, and even a lowly peon with a spare *real* would not have to seek far when the ever-recurring urge to gamble came upon him. Impromptu horse races in the street or the mad dashes of serape-draped youths bent upon impressing a señorita with the speed of their steeds offered hazards for pedestrians, but added to the animation and spontaneity of the picture.

The gaiety and lustiness of day was carried over by night to the well-lighted dance halls where bailes or fandangos provided both amusement and opportunity to promote romantic interests. Admission was usually free and from a side room El Paso brandy and assorted sweet delicacies were sold for refreshment. Frequently, the baile ended in a mad free-for-all with serious injuries resulting, but throughout such periods of bedlam, the musicians continued to play, although at a somewhat faster tempo.

In the years following New Mexico's annexation in 1846, the province grew in population and experienced a minor economic boom. The decade of the 1850's was perhaps the heyday of the Santa Fe Trail. By 1849, light spring wagons were in use to carry a regular mail to the States, and in the succeeding year heavy coaches, tightly built so they could be floated across rivers, were making monthly runs to St. Louis.

Although Indians were still troublesome on the frontier, the danger around Santa Fe itself began to recede and the capital knew a measure of security for the first time. The influence of the Church was strengthened by the arrival of Bishop Jean B. Lamy (later archbishop) who introduced reforms and encouraged establishment of schools. And the city's traditional isolation began to give way as the citizenry took up debates on statehood for New Mexico and the slavery issue. It was an exciting and vigorous time for Santa Fe, a last youthful fling before she settled into staid maturity.

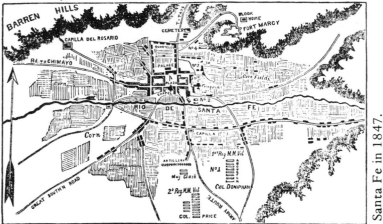

Santa Fe in 1847.

47

"TELEGRAPH" AUBRY: A RIDING MAN

Today when it is remembered, as it seldom is, that a wiry little fellow named Francois Xavier Aubry rode horseback from Santa Fe to Independence, Missouri, in less than six days, that fact makes scarcely an impression — certainly it now seems a meager achievement as compared to men rocketing to the moon. And yet, is there anyone at present with the endurance and constancy of purpose who could duplicate Aubry's performance?

»»»»

Aubry was a French-Canadian born in Quebec in 1824. Leaving home at eighteen, he wandered down to St. Louis, the chief commercial entrepot for the West, where he became a store clerk. But this menial job proved unsuitable for a youth with an appetite for adventure and boundless energy, and he soon found a way to join in the Santa Fe trade. Very quickly he gained attention by undertaking to make two trips a year to New Mexico instead of the customary one. Merchandise he carried to Santa Fe was rapidly disposed of, and the enormous profits realized allowed him to indulge a growing taste for fast, long-distance travel.

On December 22, 1847, for example, Aubry left Santa Fe headed for Independence. Five companions who trailed out with him were soon worn to a nub by the hard pace and dropped by the roadside. Harassed by a gang of robbers and set upon by Indians, he spurred ahead with a single-mindedness which also carried him through the rigors of a plains blizzard. In spite of these hindrances, Aubry maintained an astounding speed, riding several mules to exhaustion and covering the last 300 miles in three days. He galloped into Independence only fourteen days out of Santa Fe, surpassing the old record by ten and a half days.

The local paper applauded his unbelievable daring and swiftness and labelled him "Telegraph" Aubry. And never did a man work with greater zeal to live up to his nickname: the following year by racing over the same distance, New Mexico to Missouri, he completed the trip in eight days and ten hours, thereby shattering his own previous record. In September, 1848, "Telegraph" Aubry announced he would dash from Santa Fe to Independence in even shorter time. And the local *Santa Fe Republican* expressed belief he could do it because "this gentleman travels with a rapidity almost supernatural."

The new adventure was to be Aubry's supreme riding achievement. On the twelfth of the month under a yellow morning sun, he pounded out of Santa Fe carrying in his saddlebags an "Extra" run off by the *Santa Fe Republican* with news of the Territory and of Mr. Aubry himself. Keeping up a terrific pace out of the mountains and over the Great Plains, he secured fresh mounts from passing wagon trains and at other points where he had stationed them. His renowned yellow mare, Dolly, bore him 200 miles in less than twenty-six hours. For more than two-thirds of the way, he was plagued by rain and mud, but he rode on, rubbing his eyes with tobacco juice to keep awake and eating scant meals. Day and night he persevered, fording swollen streams and at one point taking up the trail on foot as a lathered horse dropped beneath him.

On Sunday evening of September 17th, with his last mount fatigued and staggering, Aubry rode into Independence. He had completed this incredible journey, a distance of 800 miles, in five days and sixteen hours, averaging 140 miles a day. On arrival he was so exhausted he had to be lifted out of his dragoon saddle and carried into a hotel. *The Weekly Reveille* declared in astonishment, "The extraordinary feat of this gentleman . . . transcends the history of travelling." And the famous freighter, Alexander Majors, wrote later, "The man who attempted to ride 800 miles in the time he did took his life in his hands. There is perhaps not one man in a million who could have lived to finish such a journey."

For Francois Aubry there were no more records to be set on the Santa Fe Trail. For a while he dabbled in the pioneering of a new road through Texas to Chihuahua, then returned to his congenial pastime of long-distance running, making several lightning trips from New Mexico to California and back. On one of these in the impoverished country west of Zuni supplies gave out and hostile Indians almost took his life. The Dolly mare, companion of so many trails, was killed by an arrow and Aubry had to eat a chunk of her to keep from starving.

On August 18, 1854, he rode into Santa Fe and dismounted in front of the Mercure Bros. Store on the south side of the plaza. From some distance away, Major Richard Weightman, a much-esteemed territorial citizen and newspaper man, observed his arrival and remarked to a friend, "Ah, there is Mr. Aubry. I must go and see him."

Proceeding to the store, he found the illustrious traveller already tipping a bottle, and after shaking hands, Aubry offered him a drink which was cordially declined. Weightman seated himself on the counter and he and Aubry conversed amicably for several minutes. The latter shortly asked what had become of Weightman's newspaper called *Amigo del Pais* and was told that it had perished for lack of subscribers. "Good thing," Aubry replied. "Such a lying paper ought to die."

The Major expressed some surprise at this and asked what was meant. "Last time I was around," Aubry said flatly, "you asked about my travels, then afterwards distorted what I'd told you and abused me."

When Weightman denied this, the little rider brought his fist heavily down on the counter and bellowed, "I say it is so."

Weightman slid off the counter and picking up a glass of liquor, dashed the contents into Aubry's face. He then stepped back and hooked thumbs in his belt. Aubry drew a revolver from his left side, but with such haste that it discharged prematurely, sending a bullet into the ceiling. By this time Weightman had produced a formidable looking Bowie knife and the two came together and grappled. Before others could pull them apart, Aubry's abdomen was ripped and both were bathed in blood. Within ten minutes, the toughest and fastest rider of the prairies was dead.

Major Weightman was afterward arrested and charged in the death of F.X. Aubry. At trial, however, he pleaded self-defense and was acquitted. Aubry was laid to rest in the parish church at Santa Fe, his funeral graced by the presence of hundreds of persons, great and small, who had admired and respected him. It was a tragic and ignoble end for a man who had courted danger all his life and whose marvelous exploits were accomplished on sheer nerve and grit.

Achaque quiere la muerte para llevarse a los mortales. Death needs no pretext to carry off the living.

BISHOP LAMY'S HAIRBREADTH ESCAPE

In the year 1850, a small stern-faced Frenchman named Jean Baptiste Lamy arrived in Santa Fe. He was the first bishop ever appointed by the Roman Catholic Church to take up duties in New Mexico.

Throughout the Spanish and Mexican periods, the province had been under the Bishop of Durango who resided almost 800 miles to the south. That was a special inconvenience for the faithful living in the Rio Grande Valley because only on rare occasions did the bishop pay them an official ecclesiastical visit. The road from the south was long and difficult, infested with hostile Apaches, and the churchmen were not eager to risk their necks.

When Bishop Lamy reached Santa Fe by stagecoach from the East, he found a monumental task awaiting him. After centuries of neglect, priests were few, churches were in disrepair, and many persons had strayed from the fold. With determination, he began at once to set things right.

It took some doing, but over the next three years he traveled back and forth across the Southwest visiting his scattered flock. By 1853, he had organized the vast Diocese of Santa Fe which encompassed all New Mexico, Arizona, and parts of west Texas and Colorado. And he summoned both priests and nuns from the East to found churches and schools. By his zeal, Lamy imparted a new spirit and energy to the work of the Church.

Late in 1866, the Bishop traveled to Rome to attend a Vatican conference. While there he seized the opportunity to recruit a number of Italian Jesuit priests to return with him to New Mexico. On the journey home, he went by way of Ohio where he enlisted a group of Sisters of

Charity. Much pleased with his band of new workers, he led the party to Missouri where they joined a wagon train just departing over the Santa Fe Trail for New Mexico.

On the following July 19, 1867, a shocking story appeared in bold type on the front page of the *New York Herald*. It read: "A wagon train was captured last Sunday near Fort Larned, Kansas by the Indians. Bishop Lamy, ten priests and six Sisters of Charity accompanied the train as passengers, en route to Santa Fe. The men were killed, scalped and fiendishly mutilated. The females were carried away captive. This information comes through reliable sources."

A priest from Topeka added further details. According to what he had heard, the Bishop had been hacked to pieces, and the priests staked out on the prairie, tortured and scalped. "Oh, the poor sisters," he wrote. "What horror to be slaves at the mercy of these savages; dragged from village to village subjected to every kind of outrage and probably to die lashed to the post of torture. Let us draw the veil over it all, and pray!"

The news was flashed around the world, and people everywhere grieved for the unfortunate victims.

Then suddenly like phantoms, the wagon train, the Bishop, the priests and sisters emerged from the great plains and entered Trinidad, Colorado. With considerable astonishment, they read in a Denver paper the account of their own massacre. How the dreadful story had started no one could say.

Yes, there had been an Indian attack upon the caravan along the Arkansas River. Several teamsters had been killed and one young sister had "died of fright" at the height of the fighting. But there was no massacre.

The Indians, probably Comanches, struck the corralled train early in the morning. They circled, and shouted, and fired a hail of arrows throughout the day. Bishop Lamy had immediately taken charge and with a pair of blazing six-guns stood in the forefront of the defenders. After seven hours of combat, the assault had been beaten back and the travelers saved.

On August 15, Lamy entered Santa Fe during a heavy rainstorm. In spite of the weather, hundreds of people rode out on horseback to meet him. Bells throughout the capital rang their welcome. The Bishop thanked his well-wishers and remarked casually that after 66 days on the trail and a close brush with death at the hands of the Indians, he felt "just a little tired."

MURDER MOST ATROCIOUS

Wanton killing has been around as long as human civilization itself. In Santa Fe during the summer of 1869 there occured a notable example — what the local press called "a murder most atrocious, a robbery most daring." The victim was James L. Collins, government official, newspaperman, and merchant.

Born in Kentucky, Collins moved to Missouri in 1819 and entered merchandising. Five years later he made an overland trip by mule train to the Southwest in the company of traders. As that life appealed to him, he became active in the growing commerce with Santa Fe and the north Mexican provinces.

By 1828 the prospering young man had established his residence in Chihuahua City. From that base he made periodic business trips to El Paso, Albuquerque, Santa Fe and even St. Louis. The pattern of his life, however, was disrupted in 1846 by the outbreak of war with Mexico. During the conflict he provided a variety of services, mainly as a guide and interpreter, to U.S. forces. In official reports, his name frequently received honorable mention.

After the war, Collins settled in New Mexico's capital and in 1852 founded the *Santa Fe Weekly Gazette*, the first paper of any permanence in the territory. He also served two terms as the local Superintendent of Indian Affairs, receiving his appointment directly from the president. His administration of that office, according to published statements, was free from the usual corruption.

James Collins was a staunch Union man, so when the Civil War broke forth he rallied to Lincoln's call. Although now in his sixties, he saw action at the battles of Valverde near Fort Craig, at Glorieta Pass, and

53

at the Peralta skirmish below Albuquerque. When General Sibley's Texans occupied Santa Fe briefly in April 1862, they seized Collins' *Gazette* and used it to print rebel proclamations.

After the war, "Colonel" Collins, as he was now known, received a presidential appointment as U.S. Depositary in Santa Fe. That meant he received and dispersed government funds to federal office holders and the military. He combined his office with a residence in an adobe building near the center of town. There, late on Saturday night of June 6, 1869, he was slain by intruders.

According the pages of his own *Gazette*, "The news spread like a prairie fire and in a few minutes the people began to assemble at the scene of the tragedy in large numbers, all lamenting the fate of the brave old gentleman who laid down his life at the post of duty."

U.S. Marshall John Pratt was called and a hurried examination of the scene revealed the story of the crime. In the dead of night, thieves had gained entrance to an interior courtyard and then with iron bars they pried open the door of the office. There they broke into a small safe which was believed to have contained the keys to a large vault in the wall.

Somewhere in the midst of their work, they aroused the Colonel from sleep. Hearing noise, he put on his slippers, lighted a candle, and taking a revolver stole quietly toward his office. As he opened the door, a shot rang out and he fell dead, with a bullet through the heart.

His assailants must have momentarily held their breaths, wondering if the sound had betrayed them. But the adobe walls evidently muffled the gunshot, and they quickly went back to work.

The vault was stacked with bundles of currency tied in wrappers. There was so much that the burglars tossed aside packets of small bills, scattering them on the floor. Next morning a quick count showed they had made away with $100,000.

The case proved very puzzling to authorities. The crime was obviously well-planned, by professional criminals it would seem. And they had clearly been familiar with the plan of Collins' office and known that he kept a large quantity of cash on hand. The mystery deepened two days later when about two-thirds of the stolen loot was found in an abandoned brewery on the north side of the city.

Although pleased that a large part of the money had been recovered, the *Gazette* proclaimed, "The crime remains to be punished by the law and never will be atoned for until the criminals hear pronounced upon them on the day of judgment the awful sentence, 'Depart from Me and prepare for the Devil and his angels'."

So far as can be determined, the culprits were never caught and Col. Collins' death went unpunished.

There is also a curious and tragic postscript to the story. Press accounts note that the victim was survived by a single child, Mrs. James M. Edgar of Santa Fe. A bare three months after the slaying of her father, Mrs. Edgar was notified that her son had been murdered on the Rio Mimbres near Silver City.

According to a letter she received from Grant County, he had been participating in a cattle drive when two of his cowboy companions killed him "in a most cruel manner." Two murders in the same family, wholly unrelated, would have to be regarded as an extraordinary coincidence.

THE COMING OF THE RAILROAD, 1880

The year 1880 was a watershed for New Mexico, as the Atchison, Topeka and Santa Fe Railway was built across the Territory bringing with it new progress and a commercial boom.

Throughout the late '70s, the AT&SF busily laid track along the route of the old Santa Fe Trail. By July 4, 1879, rails had reached Las Vegas, 65 miles east of the New Mexican capital. From that place, company engineers made plans to push on to Santa Fe, Albuquerque, and thence down the Rio Grande Valley to a point north of Las Cruces. At the latter site, the tracks would divide, one branch heading west to Deming and a link-up with the Southern Pacific, which had built eastward from California, and the other branch continuing downriver to El Paso. The completed line promised to join New Mexico's principal towns to the major markets of the nation.

From the beginning, the people of Santa Fe assumed that their town would occupy a prominent place on the main line. At the last minute, however, the engineers decided to by-pass the capital and build 18 miles to the south. Their action left Santa Feans in a state of shock. Without a railroad connection, development of the local economy would be forever hindered.

In a state of panic, community leaders went to AT&SF officials and begged for at least a feeder line running up from the main tracks at Galisteo Junction (later renamed Lamy). As an inducement, they promised to pass a bond issue to help pay the costs. The company, never eager to alienate potential customers, agreed.

By February 9, 1880, the feeder line was completed to Santa Fe. On that day two engines pulling several cars covered with flags and bunting steamed into town. The train was met by a brass military band and parade of citizens led by Governor Lew Wallace and the chief justice of the Territorial Supreme Court. Those two august officials took turns pounding in the last spike.

Flowery speeches followed, including one in Spanish by Major José D. Sena. His welcoming remarks were greeted with thunderous applause and loud toots from the locomotives.

While the coming of the railroad signaled the beginning of a new era, it also marked the close of another, more romantic period — the day of the Santa Fe Trail. The capital's look-ahead citizens were delighted to see the covered wagon replaced by the steam engine, for to them that meant progress and profits. The *Weekly New Mexican*, in its issue of February 18, 1880, fairly gloated over dawning of the Machine Age. In bold headlines it proclaimed:

SANTA FE'S TRIUMPH

THE LAST LINK IS FORGED IN THE IRON CHAIN WHICH BINDS THE ANCIENT CITY TO THE UNITED STATES

—

And The Old Santa Fe Trail Passes into Oblivion

Just over a week later, on February 27, the same paper summed up for its readers in the capital what they could expect in the future. "New Mexico has hitherto been little known in the east, but this is now changed. With easy rapid communication assured, her wonderful advantages can now be heralded to the world with a certainty that attention will be attracted. Invalids will come to recuperate, and build up exhausted constitutions, capitalists will be drawn here by the great mineral wealth of the Territory, and the pleasure seeker and tourist will come to revel in the delights of our mountain scenery."

As a maker of sound predictions, the journalist was right on target. But, of course, he could have had no idea of the magnitude of the impact both developers and tourists would have upon Santa Fe and New Mexico in the second half of the twentieth century.

VIOLENCE IN POLITICS

During the 1890s Santa Fe was rocked by what one historian has described as "the most deplorable series of murders, assassinations and tragedies ever registered in the chronicles of the capital." At the center of the storm were Francisco (Frank) Borrego and his brother Antonio.

The trouble started after the city elections of 1890. Frank Borrego, a Democrat serving as coroner, had a squabble with the County Commission, which replaced him with another Democrat, José Gallegos. Borrego was so angry that he became a Republican, taking many of his friends and relatives with him.

Later, Borrego chanced to meet Gallegos at a dance hall on San Francisco Street. Hot words passed between the two men and they adjourned outside to settle their differences with a fight. The matter got out of hand, spectators joined in the ensuing brawl, and Frank Borrego pulled a gun and shot his rival in the head.

He was at once marched off to jail. There he was chained to a post buried in the ground and soon afterward received a severe beating from the jailer, Juan Domínguez, a friend of the slain Gallegos.

Poor Borrego complained to Sheriff Francisco Chávez about his treatment. The Sheriff replied that he'd gotten just what he deserved, and to drive home the point, he administered a pistol whipping about the head. As a result of this second drubbing, Frank Borrego was temporarily blinded.

At the trial, Borrego was lucky to have Thomas B. Catron defending him. Catron was head of the Republican political machine and one of the richest and most powerful men in the Territory. On a plea of self-defense, he managed to get his client off for the killing of José Gallegos.

Now free, Frank Borrego went to Colorado to recuperate and recover his eyesight. Before departing, he swore vengeance against the men who had beaten him in jail. By May, 1892 he was back in Santa Fe.

On the 29th of that month, Francisco Chávez, who had recently left office as sheriff, was walking home after dark. Crossing the railroad bridge over the Santa Fe River at Guadalupe Church, he was felled by a hail of bullets. Neighbors running into the street failed to catch a glimpse of the assailants.

When jailer Juan Domínguez learned of the death of his former boss he was gripped by panic. However, instead of running, he decided to go looking for Borrego. "Santa Fe is not big enough for the both of us," he told friends. But his ambush, from a hiding place near the Cathedral, backfired. His first shots missed and Frank Borrego gunned him down with a Colt .45.

For this latest killing, Borrego again got off with self-defense. His attorney Catron, who had narrowly escaped an assassination attempt a short time before, proved that he was adroit in keeping fellow Republicans out of jail.

But times were tough and politics dirty. Some unscrupulous Democrats saw a chance to damage Catron's reputation by pursuing, if not actually railroading, his friend and client, Frank Borrego.

Time drifted by and at last Frank was indicted for the murder of former Sheriff Chávez. His brother Antonio and two companions, named Alarid and Valencia, were also charged in the indictment.

A 37-day trial created a sensation around the Territory. On May 29, 1895 exactly three years after the slaying of Chávez, the four accused were found guilty and sentenced to hang.

An appeal was made at once to the Territorial Supreme Court. The evidence had been circumstantial, the defendants maintaining their innocence and claiming they had been in a card game at the time of the murder. Also, the conduct of the trail had been surrounded by numerous irregularities. During the proceedings, Sheriff William Cunningham, a Democrat, was reported to have played poker with the jurors, given them cigars, and even taken them out to a nearby race track to see his horse run.

Nevertheless, the supreme court upheld the verdict. Over the next several years, the condemned men received no less than six stays of execution, two of them coming upon appeals to Presidents Cleveland and McKinley to commute the sentences.

Time finally ran out on April 2, 1897. The condemned were marched to the scaffold amid tight security. Friends had threatened to rescue them at the last moment. But the executions were carried out, although it was not certain, at the time, that justice had been done.

To this day, some historians contend that the Borregos and their friends were victims of a political conspiracy. The full truth of the affair may never be known. But the case serves as a good example of the dark and violent character of political life in Territorial New Mexico.

SANTA FE BURROS – 1895

Judge W.J. Eaton of Santa Fe was the proud possessor of two fine specimens of *Equus asinus,* commonly known to the *paisano* as burros. Hay was expensive and pasturage about town scarce, so when the Judge noticed one day a fine stand of weeds along an acequia not far from his home, the thought naturally occurred to him that his perennially hungry donkeys should be given the opportunity to clear that unsightly tangle of herbage.

Introduced to this splendid repast, the donkeys waded in jaws first. Unknown to the Judge, some fine stalks of corn were mixed with the weeds, and before long these too were devoured by the undiscriminating diners.

The ravished patch had an owner, the worthy citizen Diego Abeyta, who had artfully contrived to bring forth a few roasting ears on this neglected piece of ground. Discovering his loss, Abeyta appealed to the City Marshal and had the offending donkeys taken into custody on a charge of trespass. In due course, the long-eared criminals were sold to Juan Cisneros for $3, which the Marshal pocketed.

Judge Eaton, who was somewhat careless in keeping up with his property, finally noticed the absence of his burros. When a search turned them up in the Cisneros corral, he instituted court proceedings for recovery. A jury impaneled by Chief Justice José María García, after sitting through two days of legal battling, decided the animals in dispute rightfully belonged to Judge Eaton. Court costs were assessed against Cisneros, who was advised to retrive his $3 from the City Marshal. To the Marshal went the recommendation that he bring whatever charge he could think up against Diego Abeyta.

A city newspaper reporting upon this affair, which had aroused much controversy, pointed out that Judge Eaton came away owning the most expensive pair of burros in New Mexico, since as a result of the litigation they had brought costs on somebody of about $40 apiece. The paper neglected to mention the then well-known fact that the going price for a burro was $5.

Many years ago Charles Lummis remarked that for its size, no town on earth had more burros than Santa Fe. For three centuries the flop-eared donkey was a familiar fixture on the streets of the old capital: the bearer of wood, water, alfalfa, trunks and hide boxes, and squirmy children; and the community alarm clock, braying raucously each dawn to protest the day's work ahead. Only in the last couple of decades has Mr. Burro disappeared, the sturdy back no longer needed and his morning music gladly dispensed with. Now, he has not a single monument to his memory, as if an equine contribution to the building of New Mexico was a thing of little merit. Time conceals achievement while history rescues it, and perhaps one fortunate day, the burro will receive that belated recognition that is his due.

Alfalfa growing in the Santa Fe plaza about 1860. Governor's Palace at the left.

A street scene in old Santa Fe.

San Miguel Chapel in 1887.

East Santa Fe in the late nineteenth century.

East side of Plaza, Santa Fe.

Lincoln Avenue, Santa Fe.

SANTA FÉ

A POSTSCRIPT

Santa Fe in the twentieth century can look back on a history unequaled in richness or excitement by any other American city. The flag of Spain floated over the ancient Governors Palace twice as long as that of the United States has to date. And it is the firm stamp of this Iberian heritage that makes Santa Fe worthy of her designation as "The City Different."

Conformity dulls men's minds by excluding all but the commonplace; variety and individuality stimulate and inspire and are the sources of an extra dimension in human experience. The unique character of Santa Fe: her distinctive architecture, carefully tended historical landmarks, independent-minded and often colorful citizenry, and the jewel setting along her thin silvery bracelet of a river, exert a magnetic appeal upon all those of sensitivity and imagination who see the city for the first time. Here in the tree-shaded plaza or along narrow streets one may feel the pulse of centuries and easily call to mind pictures of the past when Santa Fe throbbed with the life of a frontier capital and Spanish soldier, mountain man, trader, and cowboy regarded her as civilization's outpost in a wide and remote land.

A SANTA FE CHRONOLOGY

1540   Francisco Vásquez de Coronado explores the Southwest.

1598   Colonization of New Mexico begun by Juan de Oñate.

1610   Santa Fe founded under the direction of Governor Pedro de Peralta.

1613   Governor Peralta assaults members of the Santa Fe clergy.

1640   Governor Luís de Rosas assassinated.

1675   Four Pueblo Indians executed in Santa Fe for murdering Spaniards, and about forty others whipped for practicing sorcery.

1680   Revolt of the Pueblo Indians and expulsion of the Spaniards under Governor Otermín from Santa Fe.

1693   General Diego de Vargas expells the Tano Indians from Santa Fe and reoccupies the old capital.

1707   Comanche and Ute Indians visit Santa Fe to make a peace treaty which is soon broken.

1710   San Miguel Church, destroyed in the Pueblo Revolt, is rebuilt.

1760   Bishop Pedro Tamarón of Durango visits Santa Fe.

1778   Juan Bautista de Anza arrives in New Mexico to become governor.

1807   Zebulon M. Pike held prisoner in Santa Fe for trespassing on Spanish territory.

1821   Independence from Spain is achieved.

1822   First wagons taken over the Santa Fe Trail.

1837   Chimayó Rebellion and murder of Governor Albino Pérez.

1846   First year of the Mexican War: Governor Manuel Armijo flees New Mexico and General Stephen W. Kearny occupies Santa Fe.

1848   F.X. Aubry makes his fastest ride from Santa Fe to Independence in a little less than six days.

1850   A formal territorial government is created for New Mexico.

1851   Jean B. Lamy becomes the first bishop of New Mexico.

1862   A Confederate army under General H.H. Sibley briefly occupies Santa Fe.

1879   Governor Lew Wallace writes a portion of *Ben Hur* in the old Palace.

1880   Construction of the Santa Fe Railroad through New Mexico.

1883   Santa Fe's Tertio-millenial Celebration.

1892   Territorial capitol building burns in mysterious fire.

1912   New Mexico becomes the 47th state of the Union.

A NOTE ON SOURCES

A writer whose subject is history is under obligation to name his sources of information, both to establish the truthfulness of his presentation and to provide guidelines for those who might wish to read further.

On the beginnings of Santa Fe see "Instructions to Governor Peralta by the Viceroy," *New Mexico Historical Review,* IV (1929); and in the same issue, Lansing B. Bloom, "When Was Santa Fe Founded." The old view that the city was originally named Villa de Santa Fe de San Francisco de Assisi has been challenged by Fray Angelico Chávez who shows that this designation was not adopted until 1823 when St. Francis was made municipal patron. *Archives of the Archdiocese of Santa Fe* (1957), p. 194.

That so much detail is available on the Church-State conflict in seventeenth century New Mexico is owing almost entirely to the research of Dr. France V. Scholes in the Inquisition Archives of Mexico City. The stories on the Peralta-Ordóñez feud and the practice of witchcraft derive from his studies, "Church and State in New Mexico, 1610–1650," *NMHR* (1936); and "The First Decade of the Inquisition in New Mexico," *NMHR* (1935).

The seige of Santa Fe during the Pueblo Revolt of 1680 has been described in many places, the account presented here being taken largely from the report of Governor Antonio de Otermín published in Charles W. Hackett, ed., *Historical Documents Relating to New Mexico, Nueva Vizcaya, and Approaches Thereto, to 1773,* vol. III.

On Governor Anza's plan to move Santa Fe consult Governor Fernando de la Concha to Jacobo Ugarte y Loyola, Santa Fe, June 20, 1778, Archivo General de la Nación, Mexico, Provincias Internas, vol. 161; and Alfred B. Thomas, *Forgotten Frontiers* (1932).

The Independence Day celebration in 1822 was described by Thomas James in his book, *Three Years Among the Indians and Mexicans* (1916). A copy of Barrerio's municipal ordinances is preserved in the Mexican Archives of New Mexico, State Records Center, Santa Fe. The assassination of Governor Albino Pérez is treated in Josiah Gregg, *Commerce of the Prairies* (1954); and in an article by Pérez' son which appeared in the *Santa Fe New Mexican,* June 15, 1901. Information on the Chaves-Armijo horserace is located in the "Manuel A. Chaves File" at the Museum of New Mexico History Library. On F.X. Aubry's famous rides see his journals published in Ralph P. Beiber, ed., *Exploring Southwestern Trails, 1846–1854* (1938); and various issues of the *Santa Fe Republican* for 1847 and 1848. Ralph Emerson Twitchell presents newspaper reports describing Aubry's death in his *Leading Facts of New Mexico History,* vol. II. The story of Lamy's experience in 1867 on the Santa Fe Trail has been recounted in several places, but most completely in Paul Horgan's *Lamy of Santa Fe* (1975). The Collins killing is described in detail in period newspapers preserved in the New Mexico State Library, Santa Fe. The Borrego affair has been the subject of several studies, most recently one by Tobias Duran, "Francisco Chávez, Thomas B. Catron, and Organized Political Violence in Santa Fe in the 1890s," *NMHR* (1984). Details concerning Judge Eaton's wayward burros appeared in the *Santa Fe New Mexican*, Nov. 2, 1895.

For general reference the reader should consult Twitchell's *Old Santa Fe*, first published in 1925 and reprinted in 1963 without needed revisions. Paul Horgan's *Centuries of Santa Fe* (1956) is a literary evocation of the mood of the old city during several periods of her history. Similarly, two significant novels capture the flavor of times past: Fray Angelico Chávez' *The Lady from Toldeo, A Novel of Santa Fe* (1960); and Willa Cather's *Death Comes for the Archbishop* (1927). Highly useful is John Sherman's, *Santa Fe, A Pictorial History* (1983).

INDEX

Abeyta, Diego, 61
Agua Fria, 9
Alarid, Mr., 59
Albuquerque, 29
Amigo del Pais, 50
Angeles, Beatriz de los, 23
Anza, Don Juan Bautista de, 29-31
Apaches, 29, 51
Arizpe, Sonora, 30-31
Armijo, Manuel, 39-45
Atchison, Topeka and Santa Fe
    Railway, 56-57
Aubry, Francois Xavier
    ("Telegraph"), 48-50

Baca, Roman, 42-43
Barreiro, Antonio, 35-37
Barrio de Analco, 30-31
Bent, Charles, 46
Borrego, Antonio, 58-60
Borrego, Francisco (Frank), 58-60
Burros, 61-62

Canyon de Chelly, 41
Catron, Thomas B., 58-59
Chaves, Manuel Antonio, 41-44
Chávez, Francisco, 58-60
Chimayó Rebellion, 39, 41
Cisneros, Juan, 61
Civil War, 53-54
Cleveland, Pres. Grover, 59
Cochití Pueblo, 30
Collins, James L., 53-55
Columbus, Christopher, 12
Comanches, 29, 52
Coronado, Francisco Vásquez de,
    9, 14
Cruz, Juana de la, 23
Cunningham, William, 59

De Vargas, Diego SEE
    Vargas, Diego de
Domínguez, Juan, 58-59

Eaton, W.J., 61-62
Edgar, Mrs. James M., 55
El Paso del Norte, 27-28

Ferdinand, King, 11
Fort Larned, Kansas, 52

Galisteo Junction SEE Lamy
Gallegos, José, 58
García, José Maria, 61
Gómara, Francisco López de, 14
González, José, 39-40
Governor's Palace SEE
    Palace of the Governors
Granada, 11-13

Hawikuh, 14
Historia General de las Indias, 14

Independence, Missouri, 48-49
Inquisition, 20, 22-23
Isabel, Queen, 11-12

James, Thomas, 32-34

Kearny, Stephen Watts, 45-46

Lamy, 56
Lamy, Jean B., 47, 51-52
Lummis, Charles, 62

McKinley, Pres. William, 59
Majors, Alexander, 49
Marcy Hill, 27
Melgares, Facundo, 34

Mendinueta, Fermín de, 30
Mercure Bros. Store, 50
Moors, 11-13

Nambé Pueblo, 17
Navajos, 29, 41
New York Herald, 52

Oñate, Juan de, 9, 28
Ordóñez, Fr. Isidro, 16-20
Otermín, Antonio de, 24-28

Palace of the Governors, 13, 20,
    26, 31, 44, 46
Pecos Pueblo, 24
Pedraza, Fr. Jerónimo, 19
Peinado, Fr. Alonso, 16
Peralta, Pedro de, 9, 11, 13-14,
    17-20
Pérez, Albino, 38-39
Pike, Zebulon, 33
Pindi Pueblo, 9
Pio, Fr., 25
Polk, Pres. James Knox, 45
Pratt, John, 54
Pueblo Rebellion, 24-28

Railroad, 56-57
Rosas, Luís de, 20

San Gabriel, 9, 11
San Juan Pueblo, 9, 22
San Miguel Chapel, 14, 20, 25-26
Sandia Mission, 20
Santa Cruz Valley, 29
Santa Fe de Granada
    (New Mexico), 14-15

Santa Fe de Granada
    (Spain), 12, 14
Santa Fe Republican, 49
Santa Fe Trail, 47, 49, 52, 57
Santa Fe Weekly Gazette, 53-54
Santo Domingo Pueblo, 16-19, 30
Scolly, John, 43
Sena, José D., 57

Tanos Pueblos, 24
Tertio-Millenial Celebration, 10
Tesuque Indians, 24-25
Tewa Indians, 9
Tirado, Fr. Luís, 17-19
Treaty of Córdova, 32

Valencia, Mr. 59
Vargas, Diego de, 28

Wallace, Lew, 57
Weekly New Mexican, 57
The Weekly Reveille, 49
Weightman, Maj. Richard, 50
Witchcraft, 22-23